Every dollar travels from person to person in a different way. But each dollar starts out in the same place—the Bureau of Engraving and Printing in Washington, D.C. Since 1862, this is where our nation's paper money has been produced. The Bureau is part of the United States Treasury Department. At the Bureau, huge printing presses run round the clock, turning out dollar bills. In twenty-four hours, ten million one-dollar bills can be printed.

Dollars are printed in big sheets of thirty-two bills. First the basic design is printed. Then the sheets are cut in half and go back to the presses for an overprinting. This second printing adds information such as the serial numbers and the Treasury seal.

As bills are made, they're checked by people and machines over and over again to make sure they are perfect.

Finally, the sheets are cut into stacks of individual bills called bricks. Bricks are sent to one of twelve banks, located in different parts of the United States, called Federal Reserve Banks.

Federal Reserve Banks, in turn, send dollars to banks in cities, small towns, and neighborhoods. From here, dollars go into circulation, to be used by people all over America: in stores, cafeterias, movie theaters, and thousands of other places—wherever money changes hands. Here's what might have happened to one dollar....

THE GO-AROUND DOLLAR

BARBARA JOHNSTON ADAMS
ILLUSTRATED BY JOYCE AUDY ZARINS

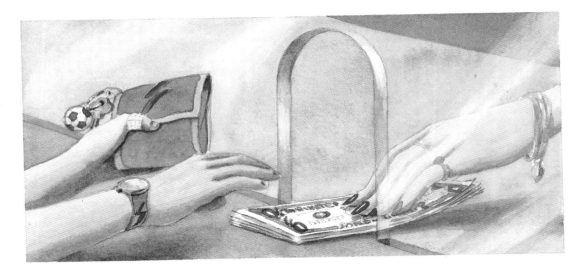

FOUR WINDS PRESS   NEW YORK

MAXWELL MACMILLAN CANADA   TORONTO

MAXWELL MACMILLAN INTERNATIONAL

NEW YORK   OXFORD   SINGAPORE   SYDNEY

To Larry, love always—B.J.A.

To my nephew, Jeremy, with love—J.A.Z.

Text copyright © 1992 by Barbara Johnston Adams
Illustrations copyright © 1992 by Joyce Audy Zarins

Four Winds Press
Macmillan Publishing Company
866 Third Avenue
New York, NY 10022

Maxwell Macmillan Canada, Inc.
1200 Eglinton Avenue East, Suite 200
Don Mills, Ontario M3C 3N1

Macmillan Publishing Company is part of the Maxwell Communication Group of Companies.
First American edition
Printed and bound in Hong Kong by South China Printing Company (1988) Ltd.
10 9 8 7 6 5 4 3 2 1
The text of this book is set in Baskerville.
The illustrations are rendered in ink, pencil, and watercolor.
Typography by Christy Hale

Library of Congress Cataloging-in-Publication Data
Adams, Barbara Johnston.
The go-around dollar / Barbara Johnston Adams ; illustrated by
Joyce Audy Zarins. — 1st American ed.
    p.   cm.
Summary: A story describing how a single dollar changes
hands, accompanied by facts about the one-dollar bill.
ISBN 0-02-700031-1
1. Dollar, American — Pictorial works — Juvenile literature.
2. Money — United States — Pictorial works — Juvenile literature.
[1. Dollar, American. 2. Money.] I. Zarins, Joyce Audy, ill.
II. Title
HG591.A63 1992
332.4'973—dc20   90-26269

The United States government has laws about the way dollar bills can be shown. For instance, a dollar drawn as an illustration for a book must be in black and white, not in full color. A dollar must also be shown either larger than one and one-half times the size of a real dollar, or smaller than three-quarters the size of a real dollar.

As Matt and Eric were walking home from school one day...

It is hard to know how many dollars are lost in one day. It's easy to drop a dollar because it weighs so little. About 490 one-dollar bills make a pound.

A portrait of George Washington, first president of the United States, is on the front of every one-dollar bill. Only people who are no longer alive can have their pictures on American money.

Matt offered to buy Eric's shoelaces for the dollar.

"Do they really glow in the dark?"

Dollar bills are used to buy things, pay back money that was borrowed, or pay for a service, such as a bus ride. There is a notice on each dollar that makes this clear: "This note is legal tender for all debts, public and private."

Eric used the dollar to buy some bubble gum...

G 90445557 ★

The front of every dollar has a long number in green ink, which appears in two different places. This is called the serial number. No two dollars have the same serial number. If a dollar is damaged while it is printed, it is replaced by a bill with a star where the last letter of the serial number would usually be. These bills are called star notes.

...and Jennifer received the dollar as part of her change from a five-dollar bill.

If dollars are in water a short time, they usually aren't damaged. They can't be ripped easily, either. This is because dollars are printed on especially strong paper made of cotton, linen, and silk. If you look closely, you can see the red and blue silk threads.

Jennifer went to a flea market and bought a funny hat from Rob with the dollar. At a booth near Rob's, a ticket seller was handed an odd-looking dollar bill.

The formula for the black and green inks used to print dollars is a secret known only by the Bureau of Engraving and Printing. The secret is important; it keeps people from making fake, or counterfeit, bills exactly like the real ones.

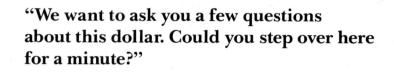

"We want to ask you a few questions about this dollar. Could you step over here for a minute?"

Sometimes people called counterfeiters *do* make fake money. But it's very hard to make a dollar that looks and feels like a real one. When counterfeiters are caught, they're fined and sent to jail.

Back at home, Rob asked his sister Kathy to do a chore for him....

When a dollar changes hands, many people don't realize they're holding the Great Seal of the United States. The two sides of the Seal, an official symbol of our country, are shown in circles on the back of every one-dollar bill. One circle has an eagle in it; the other, a pyramid with an eye. The bald eagle, our national emblem, is holding arrows and an olive branch. The arrows stand for war and the olive branch for peace. The eagle faces the olive branch, which means the United States wants peace, not war. The pyramid stands for strength and growth; the eye, spiritual values.

"Come back here, Biscuit!"

Sometimes dollars are accidentally burned, chewed by animals, or torn. The Treasury Department will replace a bill if more than half of the original remains. If less than half remains, a government official must inspect the dollar before replacing it.

Kathy thought about different ways to spend the dollar.

Lots of people say they see pictures of tiny owls or spiders near the corners of dollar bills. But the Bureau of Engraving and Printing says there are no such creatures on our money.

FEDERAL RES
THE UNITED STAT

WASHINGTON

ONE DOLLAR

Secretary of the Treasury.

One-dollar bills wear out in about eighteen months because they are passed from person to person so often. Banks collect worn-out bills and send them to one of the Federal Reserve Banks. There they are shredded by machine into little pieces too small to be put together again. But once in a while, people will keep a dollar because it has special meaning for them.

Great Seal of the United States

Federal Reserve seal and letter

serial number